"26 miles across the sea,
Santa Catalina is a-waiting for me,
Santa Catalina, island of romance.
Romance, romance, romance."

Printed in the United States

Sierra Printers, Inc.
Bakersfield, California

ISBN 0913056-13-8

Library of Congress Catalog Card 93-71599

First Printing

CATALINA!

"....Wish you were here."

c. 1947

by ray & jo miller

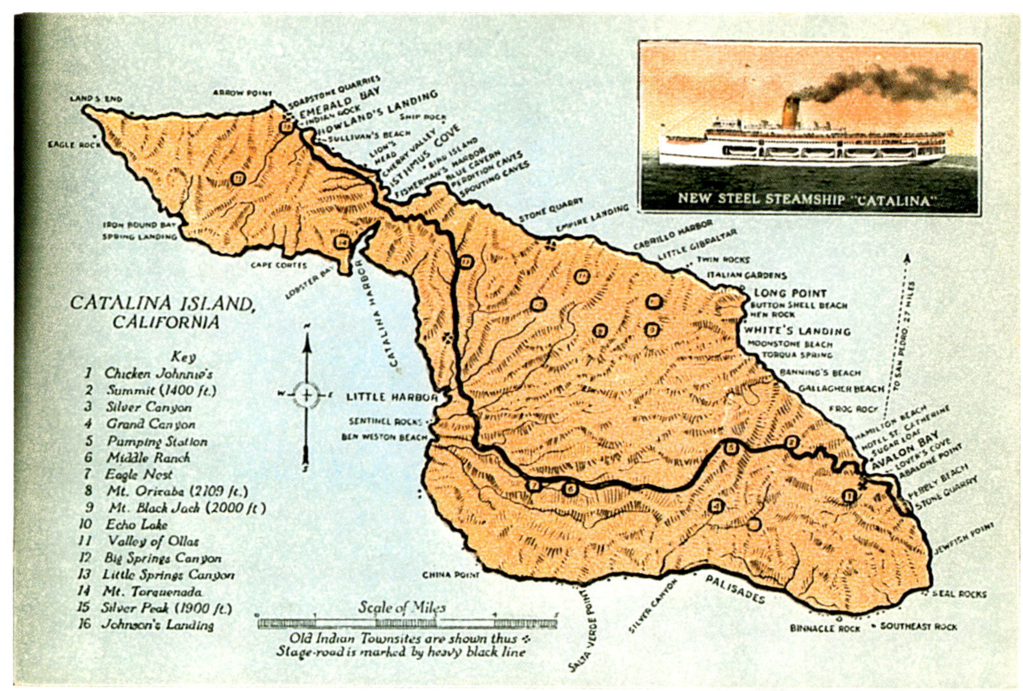

Located 22 miles from San Pedro or Long Beach, and 26 miles from Newport, Santa Catalina is one of eight Islands comprising the Channel Islands group off the coast of Southern California. Its windward side is windy and barren with only a few rocky coves, but its leeward side is pleasant, with many inviting beaches. Only 22 miles long, and 7 miles wide, Santa Catalina is the site of Avalon, the only municipality on any of these Islands.

Juan Cabrillo claimed Santa Catalina island for Spain on October 7, 1542 under the name "San Salvador". Renamed Santa Catalina in 1602, it later became part of Mexico whose Governor, Pio Pico granted the Island to Tomas M. Robbins of Santa Barbara in 1846. Although Robbins recorded his grant deed in July of 1846. it was not until the treaty of Guadalupe/Hidalgo in 1848 that his US ownership of the land was confirmed. Then, although his claim stated that he planned to use the land for farming, within two years he had sold the Island for $10,000! By 1858, quarter-shares had been sold, (the most inexpensive of which went for only $500), but by the end of 1866, ownership of the entire Island was regained by James Lick.

Twenty years later, in 1887, the Lick interests again sold the whole island, this time to George R. Shatto. When Shatto bought the Island, a small group of squatters had already located here at what was then known as "Timms Landing". It is believed that it was Shatto's sister who suggested the name "Avalon" (from Tennyson's "Idyls of the King") as a welcome improvement. Shatto then began the sale of residential lots, and built a pier and a hotel, but when the Bannings purchased his interests, the community still numbered under 100.

In 1892, after only five years, Shatto sold the entire Island to the Banning brothers of Wilmington, California, commencing a period of greater growth. The Bannings laid out the town, built roads, and contributed much to Avalon's progress. Their ships brought water here to be stored in tanks on upper Metropole Street. Reservoirs have now been built to collect rainfall, our major source of fresh water. In addition, seawater is provided on separate lines to flush toilets.

The Santa Catalina Island Company, incorporated by the Bannings in 1894 to sub-divide their Island, met with initial sucess, but then suffered a devastating fire in 1915 which wiped out a substantial portion of Avalon including the fine old Hotel Metropole.

"Arrival of the Steamer at Avalon" Circa 1911

By 1910 Avalon's population had grown to several hundred, and, following an election held in June of 1913, in which 238 of the residents voted FOR, and 132 opposed Incorporation, the new City of Avalon was born. Its population grew steadily from 586 in 1920 to about 2100 by 1940, and has remained stabile since then, limited by the available housing.

In 1919, William Wrigley Jr, a Chicago businessman who had established the successful Wrigley Chewing Gum Company, was induced to invest in the foundering development project. When he arrived to look over his holdings early in 1920 (he reportedly had not previously seen Catalina Island), Wrigley so liked what he found that he immediately bought out his partners, and ended the sale of building lots here. Consequently, land values in tiny (only one-square-mile) Avalon are high; other than the few lots occasionally released by the Santa Catalina Island Company, only those that had previously been sold are ever available for resale!

c. .1908

From the beginning, when the local Indians paddled their hollowed-out log canoes back and forth, travel to Catalina has depended on boats. As the small boats became larger ships with open decks, passengers gathered outdoors at the stern to enjoy a view of the San Pedro waterfront as their boat departed for Catalina. Then, as the ship neared Avalon, they would rush to the bow (above right) to also enjoy the incoming view of Avalon.

c. 1907

Coming ashore in Avalon, (below), they would "run the gauntlet" formed by locals and overnighters.

c. 1908

c. 1930

The "Santa Catalina Island Steamer Terminal" was subsequently replaced with a new terminal in San Pedro. The building is now the home of the Catalina Island Freight Line.

c. 1931

Most passengers are unaware that the rock, of which the breakwater was constructed, virtually all came from a quarry on Catalina Island.

c. 1950

Speedboats would generally encircle the incoming steamers, adding to the passengers' excitement.

c.1950

"Welcoming crowds gather to greet the daily arrival from the mainland. In Avalon, tiled Fountain Plaza becomes a place where the realism of everyday life is suddenly unimportant."

(promotional text from this card)

Dear Papa:

"This is the steamer we came back on from Catalina Island. We are going to motor to San Diego Monday and from there down to Mexico. We are all fine, having a glorious time".

June 4, 1924

c. 1924

c. 1932

Tired, but happy, visitors depart Avalon harbor. The building in upper right is Mt. Ada, the home built by William Wrigley, Jr..

Steamship "Avalon," Sugar Loaf Rock,
Casino and Hotel St. Catherine
Catalina Island, California

c. 1925

Avalon looking East, showing Terraces, Catalina, Ca
1907

"Came here yesterday. Leave this afternoon for Los Angeles. Just beyond the headland in the picture we found some pretty sand onyx which we have had cut into gems. Aunt Mattie and Uncle John are with us. All is well. With love,"

Father & Mother

September 28, 1907

Avalon Bay circa 1919

Avalon Bay circa 1927

Abalone Point circa 1923

Avalon Bay circa 1938

Dearest Mary,
"We are fine and dandy, and I forgot to call up Ray.
I tried to Monday but they did not answer.
Have a fine time."
Love,
Pa
April 23, 1907

c. 1907

c. 1924

'....Catalina is fascinating!....'
Frank
April 24. 1925

c. 1924

About this time, terraces were cut into the hillside (center) on which houses were later to be built.

c. 1907

c. 1930

c. 1911

Dear Louise,
"Today we went around the island in a launch. It was quite rough but we enjoyed it just the same."
Paul

Sept. 23, 1911

c. 1922

Dear George,
"It is quite hot here, and I think that Alice has been warm for once!"
Paul
June 21,1922

c. 1912

Dear Elta,
"This is a delightful (place), and I have been having a fine time and wish that you were here to help enjoy. Why don't you come over this summer?"
Beaulah
June 16, 1912

Dear Maude,
"I'm thinking of you while I am here on this pretty spot in the Pacific. My aunt is with me and we are just getting ready to take a ride on the "glass bottom boat"
Elizabeth

July 11th, 1915

c. 1915 Later this year, the fine old Hotel Metropole would be destroyed by fire.

c. 1915

By this time, Pleasure Pier had been constructed.

c. 1908 Steamer *"CABRILLO"*

Hello Charlie,
"Just arrived at Catalina today and am going to stay a week. This is the boat I came over on."
Frank

July 26, 1908

Hello Harry,
"We shall leave in about a half hour for L.A. on the boat, "AVALON" pictured here".
Marguerite

August 6, 1928

c.1928 Steamer *"AVALON"*

The *Magic Isle* was employed in the late 1940's as a cross-channel carrier. Local residents affectionately referred to the ship as the *"Tragic Pile"*.

c. 1950

C-46 STEAMER "CATALINA", CATALINA ISLAND, CALIFORNIA

CATALINA

1A-H538

Jo,
"We came over here two days ago on this boat. Lovely trip, and this Island is beautiful."
Alice R.

September 2, 1935

c. 1935

Queen of the fleet was the steamer *Catalina* which was removed from service in the mid-sixties. The ship was then vandalised and is no longer serviceable.

From the late '40's on, fast speedboats carried passengers out to meet the incoming Steamers.

c. 1940

"Aquaplaning" meant enjoying a ride on a board being pulled by a speedboat.

c.1927

Despite this card's caption, the view is not of the yacht club. Rather, it is the St. Catherine hotel at Descanso beach in the background.

c. 1940

Dear Sadie & Arthur,
"All is well and we are certainly enjoying Catalina."
Love.
Aunt Mary

April 25, 1940

c. 1940

By 1940, people were performing interesting stunts on their aquaplanes.

This scene is from a card postmarked on March 7, 1906..

It is a look at the "Arrival of Cabrillo at Avalon, Cal.", and shows not only the many people who enjoyed Avalon at the time, but also presents a view of Sugarloaf, site of the present Casino.

Dear Sister,
"I am over here today . A party of 20 came and we are having a fine time. We had dinner at the big hotel."
Mary
Dec 19, 1910

c.1910

c. 1912

c. 1905

c.1912

Dear Mary,
"We just got in some sightseeing on the glass bottom boat. Hope you all are well."
Mrs. Selby

March 14, 1912

Dear Earl,
"We are sitting out here looking out on the ocean, Wish you all were here. I think that you had better come out."
Love,
Mother

Oct. 12, 1911

c:1911

Dear Percie,
"I am having a fine time here, the scenery is beautiful."
Lovingly,
Nellie

July 23. 1914

c:1914

Uncle Ted,
"I'm here for a holiday, it's a beautiful place"
William,

Aug. 26, 1927

c. 1927

Dear Aunt Rose,
"Blanche and I are having a wonderful time. We had hoped you would stay and come over here with us."
Fred

July 18. 1928

c. 1928

The *Avalon* arrives at the steamer pier shortly after construction of the new Casino.

The *Catalina's* arrival was greeted with noise, excitement, and pandemonium.

c. 1936

The *Betty O.* was an early sightseeing boat on which daylight cruises to nearby locations were followed with an evening trip to see the flying fish.

c. 1924

Passengers aboard the *Betty O.* enjoyed their view of Descanso Canyon and the St. Catherine Hotel.

c. 1928

"Catalina Flyer, the greatest illuminated boat of its size, and the original searchlight boat. It makes the Flying Fish dance the Tango, one of the greatest sights ever seen from a boat"

Catalina Excursion Company

c. 1914

"Very beautiful here and I am enjoying my stay very much. I want to take this trip one evening to see the flying fish. It is a [rare] sight."
Martha

August 5, 1934

c. 1934

c. 1928

In Catalina waters the famous flying fish (12 to 22 inches long) fly as much as 40 miles per hour for distances as great as 300 yards only to drop back into the water when their wings become dry.

An early publisher's. whimsical view of Catalina's famous flying fish, which actually were well under two feet in length.

c. 1915

Dear Charlie,
"My vacation is almost over and I have had a fine time. I have been out rowing and fishing every day. I caught one yellowtail, one barracuda, and eight rock bass. Wish you had been here to go out with me."
Frank

June 4, 1909

c. 1909

Dear Bro.,
"Thought that we would take a few days outing. This is a nice place, so many people live in tents here. We are staying at the Pacifica Hotel and can look out over the ocean from our window."
C. L.

June 7, 1912

c. 1912

Many visitors worried about climbing the narrow stairway to the top of Sugarloaf, and gladly paid a few cents to have a local boy escort them.

c. 1910

c. 1907

Sugarloaf rock was not an island.. Although it appears so in most photos, it could be approached by a low rocky isthmus,

A favorite trip with visitors (besides climbing the stairway to the top of Sugarloaf) was a boat trip to the rocks near its base. From here there was an excellent view of the town .

c. 1908

The beautiful Hotel Metropole, the town's principal landmark, can be seen just right of center on this card postmarked May 26, 1910.

c. 1910

Peter Gano built Holly Hill House (right foreground) in 1895, supposedly for a bride awaiting his return. It is said that while he was working on it, *she* married someone else!

c. 1909

c. 1912

c. 1915

Around 1915, the large rock point inshore from Sugarloaf was removed, the site cleared, and a 90' wide by 45' high dance pavilion was erected.

Dear Kay,
"Swimming is keen here. When will you be back?"
Bill

Aug. 17, 1925

c. 1925

This pavilion remained until 1927 when it was removed to make room for the present one. Its steel skeleton was then erected at the Bird Park to become the world's largest avaiary.

"Sister Katie and I are here today [we had] the grandest trip over. We came here by train and steamer."
Terry

August 25, 1934

c. 1934

During construction of the new Casino in 1929, it became apparent that its towering 140 foot height would dwarf the adjacent Sugarloaf. The rock was then removed.

"Focal point of indoor fun is the $2,000,000 Casino"

from this Union 76 postcard

c. 1950

An artist's conception of the new two million dollar Casino. 180 feet in diameter and 140 feet in height, it contains a 1200 seat theater auditorium and a circular ballroom in which up to 6500 people are said to have danced at the same time.

c. 1930

c. 1950

"The gorgeous Catalina Island Casino is a two million dollar "Palace of Pleasure" located midway between Hotel St. Catherine and the town of Avalon. It is the only building of its size in the world erected on a full circular plan "

from this 1950's postcard

The walls of the theater auditorium still feature the stylish murals which were painted in 1929.

c. 1932

c: 1940

The illuminated Casino was highlighted by a similarly decorated walk which provided a bright entry. Searchlights on the hill light the walls of the building and remain to this day, but the "Romance Promenade" has now been removed.

Music was a way of life in the 'thirties and 'forties. The huge Casino ballroom was open to the public and orchestras played nightly. Many of the major "swing" bands such as the Jimmy Dorsey Orchestra played there as well as Alvino Rey, Freddy Martin, Kay Keyser, Benny Goodman, Bob Crosby, and many others.

People enjoyed ballroom dancing and an evening excursion to Catalina with a midnight steamer return to San Pedro was a popular entertainment.

Not only was there music at the Ballroom, but strolling Mariachi bands filled the streets of Avalon serenading arriving visitors and then again as they departed.

c. 1939

An attractive tiled stucco building was built at the entrance to the illuminated path. Although the name "Casino Way" was later changed, it is still used locally.

Lois,
"Was here today. Great place. Regards to all,"
unsigned

June 30, 1910

c. 1910

The Pilgrim's Club, built of wood and stone, was reputedly a gambling hall which stood near the foot of Marilla Street. It too was destroyed by the major conflagration of September of 1915.

c. 1918

In 1915, a disastrous fire virtually destroyed Avalon and many hotels were lost. The New Hotel Catalina claims to be the first to be built after that fire.

c. 1938

The Hotel Atwater was built by the Santa Catalina Island Company. In "downtown" Avalon it was a handsome addition to the town.

c. 1909

The Hotel Metropole was constructed by William Shatto soon after he purchased the island in 1887 intending to develop it as a residential sub-division. Recognizing the need for a major attraction if he was to successfully develop the land, he constructed a pier, laid out and sold some lots, and built the town's first large hotel.

The fine old wooden building soon became a focal point for activity in Avalon and for almost 20 years, it not only housed the town's visitors, but also served as its social center.

c. 1903

Dear Lil,
"Wish you were here, this is the lovliest place this side of Minnetonka. I went away up in the hills this AM and played base-ball. Then came back and went swimming. I am all sunburned."
unsigned

July 10, 1913

The Bannings, owners of Santa Catalina Island, built their summer home in then-remote Descanso Canyon.

c. 1924

The St. Catherine Hotel was built in Descanso Canyon, just beyond the Casino. It was started by the Banning brothers in 1918 to replace the destroyed Hotel Metropole, but upon his arrival in 1920 during its construction, Mr. Wrigley added a new wing increasing the size to 160 rooms. The building became a popular destination until World War II when it was commandeered by the Merchant Marine for use as a training facility. Although it later continued operating for several years, it was demolished about 1966.

c. 1936

By 1936, a pier had been added, making the St. Catherine more accessible to boaters.

c. 1924

The elaborately furnished lobby of the St. Catherine featured a large fireplace and a baby grand piano on which entertainment was frequently provided.

c. 1914

The Grand View hotel, another wooden building, stood at the corner of Crescent and Marilla. It too was destroyed in the 1915 fire. The El Encanto shops and restaurant now occupy the site.

c. 1908

In 1908, Catalina Avenue already featured Eucalyptus trees, several of which survive to this day.

c. 1910

By 1910, Avalon had become a "tent city" with any relatively substantial buildings limited to its front street.

c. 1910

Clusters of tents, the most well known those of Island Villas, accommodated visitors who did not chose the more elegant facilities of the Metropole.

Dear Jewel,
We just got here and are in for a week of quiet and rest. While there are lots of people here, it is very quiet."
Maria

September 4, 1908

c. 1908

The Island Villa accommodations were simple, but adequate. The units were provided with cots, dressers, and chairs. Community facilities were offered.

"Here is where I am staying for this trip. Had a fine afternoon and it is a beautiful place."
L.

August 7, 1910

c. 1910

Early communication from the Island to the mainland was by letters carried by the steamers. Later carrier pigeons were tried, but it was not until this wireless station was built that reliable communications were provided.

c.1907

This, the first building of the Tuna Club, was destroyed in the 1915 fire as were the buildings of the MiraMar, another rooming house and Pard Mathison's boat yard on the beach just west of it.

c.1910

Founded in 1898 by Dr. Charles Frederick Holder to conserve the Catalina fishery, membership in the Tuna Club is limited to those who have captured a fish of specified size and weight with rod and reel of stipulated lightness. Many well-known people have become Members, including Winston Churchill, and Presidents Theodore Roosevelt and Grover Cleveland.

The Club was rebuilt in essentially the same place after the fire, and operates in that location today. Visible in the distance directly over this building is St. Catherine's Roman Catholic church, now a private home.

c. 1920

The Catalina Island Yacht Club was constructed on the site of the former boatyard.. The Club has functioned continuosly since then except for the years 1942-1945 when the United States Merchant Marine Service used it as a school.

c. 1926

In 1924 the all-male membership of the Tuna Club, also desiring a social Club, established the Catalina Island Yacht Club. Limiting itself to 180 family Members, it has a long waiting list. Many celebrities became members, among them James Cagney, Johnny Weismuller, Hal Roach, Rudolf Valentino, and Richard Arlen.

The lighthouse on the roof of the Yacht Club is only ornamental and serves no formal navigational purpose

c. 1930

c. 1908

Above is the the first of three "bath houses" that were built in Avalon. These buildings functioned as a changing room for those who wished to swim. Later the building was modified (below) with a new roof, and an enclosed entry.

c. 1910

"Have just been in swimming here and Della and I are now going to bowl a game. I scored 148 yesterday. Great time:"
unsigned

August 24, 1911

c. 1911

This, the second of three bathouses, replaced the earlier small building. Also a wooden structure, it too was destroyed in the 1915 fire.

The third major bath house was located at the easterly side of the bay. Before being severely damaged by a mid-fifties storm and dismantled, it was employed as a seafood restaurant.

c. 1940

THE OCEAN STRAND IS HAPPY-LAND
AVALON, CATALINA ISLAND, CALIFORNIA

c. 1935

c. 1906

Summer visitors enjoyed the narrow beaches of Avalon (and they still do). The uncomfortable small beach rocks are now covered to the water's edge with sand barged over each summer from the mainland.

c. 1912

c. 1930

Dear Fred,
"Can you spot me here on the beach? I'm spending the week here."
Jean

July 15, 1940

c.1940

Seth,
"These are some of the fish caught off this coast. This is a beautiful State. Its production astonishes me."

October 11, 1910

c. 1910

Louis,
"How would you like to be out here, ducks by the hundreds all over this island."
Tafel

June 25, 1908

c. 1908

c. 1906

c. 1903

The Sun Fish is rarely seen anymore, but was fairly common when, on July 27, 1903, this huge specimen was caught.

A Five-Ton Catch of Albacore, W
Santa Catalina Island, C

d and Reel
nia

Harry,
"We are taking a little trip. At the Island for a few days. It's the prettiest place, climate ideal.. Going out on a glass bottom boat this afternoon"
Mr. & Mrs. L.H.

June 11, 1914

c. 1914

The Amphitheater, in recent times to become known as "Avalon Bowl", was built in the early 1900's to provide a location in which outdoor concerts by the Santa Catalina Island Company Band could be held.. Later, as its popularity grew, mainland artists visited the Island and performed there as well. The bowl and the seats have been demolished, but the iron railings and the concrete tiers can still be seen.

"at the beach. Wish you were here."
E.M.B.

June 7, 1909

c. 1909

Patrons not only enjoyed the concerts, but also the superb view of Sugarloaf.

Dear Mary,
"We all are having a fine time. I took this ride one day. We went boat riding this morning early then swimming."
unsigned

August 8, 1911

c.1911

The "Island Mountain Railway" was built by the Island Company about 1905 as another "attraction". Departing from the amphitheater, (preceding page), passengers were carried to the summit of what is now called Buena Vista Point for an impressive view of Lovers Cove. The finicular railroad was dismantled about 1915, but its former route can still be seen in Avalon.

c. 1912

There is a long and interesting history of aviation at Catalina Island. On May 10. 1912, Glenn Martin made the first water-to-water flight from Newport to Catalina Island in an airplane very similar to this one.

c. 1935

By about 1935, everything was "up-to-date" at Catalina!

c. 1932

By the early thirties, an airport had opened for seaplanes flying regularly between the mainland and Catalina. An unusual feature was a turntable on which planes could be rotated as they entered and left the water. The terminal building has been razed, the hanger dismantled and reassembled at the Airport-In-The-Sky, and the site is now that of Hamilton Cove, a condominium development.

At about this same tiime, the attractive "sombrero" fountain was constructed.

c. 1932

c. 1908

"Sea bathing" in 1908 was much as it is today; mostly standing and talking; occasionally actually swimming.

Despite its caption, since the steamer has not yet arrived, the boys are apparently simply enjoying themselves by high-diving off the steamer pier.

c. 1925

c. 1928

Many Island kids would "dive for coins" They would meet the incoming steamers and encourage visitors to throw small coins into the water. Then they would dive to recover them and not many visitors could resist the novelty. This activity ceased in 1966 when the *steamer Catalina,* was replaced with smaller passenger vessels.

c. 1928

"In spite of everything you say, we are having a swell time, so the laugh's on you, Harvey. Going to see the flying fish tonight."
Ed & Ellen

September 5, 1939

c. 1939

The Sugarloaf Pavilion was dismantled in 1927 to make room for the new Casino. It's steel skeleton was then erected at the new Bird Park where it formed the framework for what was then the world's largest aviary.

c. 1936

The giant cage was 110 feet in diameter and 90 feet in height. It housed several hundred rare and exotic birds.

c. 1939

CATALINA ISLAND BIRD PARK—BLACK AND WHITE SWANS. BRAZILIAN WHISTLING TREE DUCKS IN FOREGROUND

Within the giant aviary, a landscaped pond provided a suitable environment for the waterfowl.

THE CATALINA BIRD PARK HAS THOUSANDS OF RARE BIRDS

Hello Elva,
"Are starting for this place in a few minutes. Wish you were here to go along. Maybe you will some of these days."
Brig, Mary & Eloise

June 30, 1934

c. 1934

Bird Park housed one of the world's foremost collections of exotic birds. Up to 6500 birds were gathered by the Island Company starting about 1930, but in 1966 the Park was closed, the birds transferred to the Los Angeles Zoo.

c. 1926

Mt. Ada (named for Mrs. Wrigley), is the former home of William Wrigley, Jr. who bought the island in 1919. Arriving here with his wife in 1920, the site was selected for their 22 room summer home. Upon the death of his son, Philip, the house was bequeathed to the University of Southern California, and is now operated as an inn.

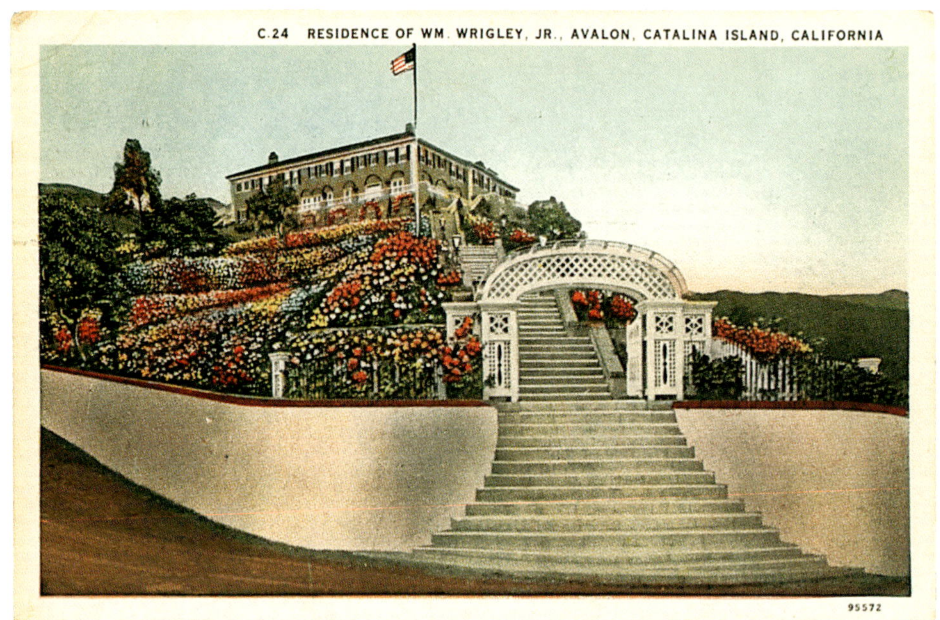

Tom,
"Having a good time on Catalina"
H. H.

June 4, 1930

c. 1930

Most visitors view the Wrigley home only from the streets below and are therefore unaware of its beauty.

c. 1928

This is the former home of Philip Knight Wrigley, William's son, who took over the operations of the Santa Catalina Island Company upon his father's death in 1932. "P.K" died in 1967, and the home is now occupied by *his* son, William.

c. 1928

D. M. Renton, builder of the Casino and many other improvements, was the Wrigleys' principal architect and engineer. His house is now privately owned.

c. 1938

Initially, Avalon was a tent city and small lots were sold, but afterward, came more substantial homes. Many of these were constructed over the original tent platforms. Lacking conventional foundations, they led to the term "on the flats".

c. 1935

The home of author Gene Stratton Porter on Catalina Street is now the Catalina Bible Church.

c. 1935

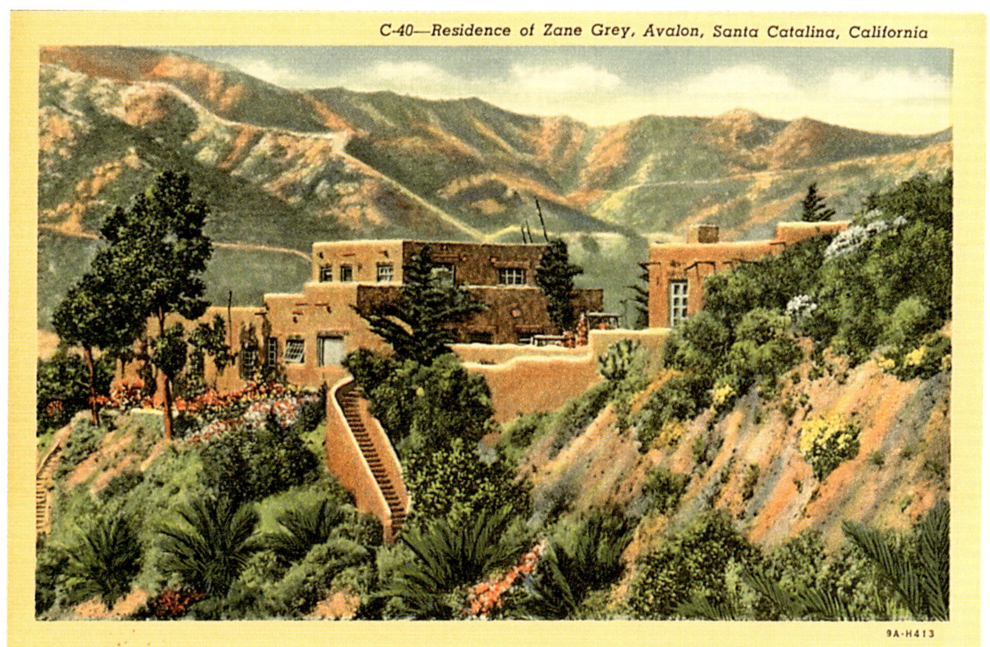

The home of writer Zane Gray, built along Indian lines. is situated on a knoll overlooking Avalon Bay. It has now been converted to an excellent hotel.

c. 1928

Avalon's High School building was presented to the City by the Island Company and replaced an earlier one-room schoolhouse on Whittley Avenue.

Hello Mother.
"Am out here to-day. Going to San Diego tomorrow. Having fun in Catalina."
Rudy

May 15, 1911

c. 1911

c. 1904

As the town became more popular, Avalon's beaches became crowded with small boats parked onshore..

c. 1911

To raise operating revenue and at the same time, reduce the congestion, a pier was built parallel to the beach and a fee charged for arriving boats.

c. 1915

Pleasure Pier has been rebuilt several times. In this version, a ticket booth for the glass bottom boats was erected between the shaded benches.

c. 1939

This pavilion was built by the Bannings and soon became a community center; Initially, dances and concerts were held there, but by the 1940's the Avalon High School basketball team played its games within. It was torn down in the early 1960's to make room for the new Pavilion Lodge which now occupies the site.

Crescent Avenue was still an unpaved road when, by 1914, electric lights had been installed.

c. 1914

c. 1908

Crescent Ave. and Harbor Avalon, Santa Catalina Island Cal.

Crescent Avenue was quiet in 1908, and the long-forgotten Hotel Windsor at the right had yet to be destroyed in the 1915 fire.

1612 - Street Scene at Avalon, Santa Catalina Island, Cal.

"We are on our vacation at Catalina. Avalon is sheer heaven."
Emma

Aug. 16, 1917

c. 1917

This 1917 card was reproduced soon after in sepia by the General Electric Company promoting the use of their Edison Mazda lamps in the new street lights.

c. 1927

Chimes Tower was donated to the people of Avalon by Mrs. Wrigley in 1926. The 45 foot high reinforced concrete Tower is a counterpart of the unfinished Hasan Tower at Rabat in Morocco which was built about 1200 AD. It houses a rare Deagan 20 pipe Tower Chimes Set, whose Westminster chimes are clock-activated and mark the time every 15 minutes. The open side of the tower has now been closed to provide better acoustics.

c. 1926

The view from the upper Tee on hole number 8 of Avalon's golf course is spectacular.

c. 1920

The Avalon course is believed to be one of the earliest in California. Initially it featured sand greens, but in about 1925, it was upgraded to 4645 yard par 66 and subsequently became the home of the Bobby Jones Tournament. Following WW II, the course was reduced to nine holes at 2085 yards, par 32.

c. 1948

c. 1910

On arriving at Avalon, visitors were greeted by friends, or they could accept transportation to hotels in horse-drawn surreys. They were also able to buy hunting licenses, and tickets on stage coach rides to the interior, or rent saddle horses at a ticket booth (left) adjacent to the terminal.

c. 1912

The Aquarium was another attraction offered visitors to Avalon. After many alternative uses, the building was demolished in the 1980's and a new building constructed which is presently a restaurant.

c. 1925

STREET SCENE. CATALINA ISLAND, CALIFORNIA.

In the 1920's, the St. Catherine hotel used a Model T Ford bus to carry passengers between the hotel and the steamer terminal. (original postcard black & white).

5503. Stage Road, Santa Catalina Island, California.

c. 1912

The stage coach ride traveled up the mountain to the Farnsworth Loop about two miles from the terminal and returned, or else continued on to the Isthmus.

c. 1935

In the 1930's, visitors could enjoy a stroll on a boardwalk extending to Lovers Cove or a sightseeing drive to Pebbly Beach.

c. 1940

By 1940, open-air lories were provided for transportation to the St. Catherine Hotel in nearby Descanso Canyon.

Joe,
"We are well"
J.W.

Nov. 21, 1907

c. 1907

In 1907 Avalon's sea gulls were well thought of. Today they are a minor nuisance.

c. 1910

A popular activity was that of seeking moonstones, (a feldspar stone with a pearly luster) at Moonstone Beach, just west of Avalon.

c. 1908

500 pound tuna were not impossible in the early days. This very large fish was caught, under Tuna Club rules, with rod and reel.

c. 1947

The marlin is one of the most exciting sport fish. In 1947, the *average* was about 350 pounds, the largest caught until then weighed 446 pounds.

"...have seen the submarine gardens and also the fine fellow on the other side. This card being mailed 27 miles from the mainland!"
Will

May 18, 1920

c. 1920

"Old Ben" was a harbor seal who became tame and who could be fed by hand. He survived for many years, and was reportedly still around in 1945. A commemorative statue to Old Ben has been placed at the end of the mole.

c.1904

The "Catalina glass bottom boat" originated when an enterprising local modified his rowboat for the purpose. Soon there was a whole fleet of these, and as their popularity spread, larger boats, with similar glass viewing bottoms were built. This one could carry about 25 people.

c.1907

The glass bottom *Empress* and the similar *Emperor* were operated by the Meteor Boat Company. They were used not only for viewing the submarine gardens, but they also made daily runs to the Seal Rocks east of Avalon.

c. 1907

The *Cleopatra* could accomodate about 40.

Dear Folks,
"Enjoying a splendid trip to Catalina. Sure is pretty."
Ed

Dec. 29, 1938

c.1938

The *Phoenix,* built in 1931, carries 156 passengers. It has been in continuous service every summer since then.

"The Submarine Gardens contain more than thirty varieties of Kelp, and as many kinds of fish. This strange and wonderful under sea life may be viewed to the depth of 75 feet, owing to the remarkably clear waters about Avalon, as the large passenger boats with plate glass bottoms glide slowly over the gardens."

METEOR BOAT COMPANY

c. 1910